Habakkuk

A Dig In Bible Study

Susan Cady

Table of Contents

WELCOME!

Welcome to Dig In: Habakkuk!

If you are new to a Dig In study please know that these studies are designed to meet you where you are. Whether you are new to studying God's Word or a seasoned student of the Word, this study is for you. We will follow six steps to study each passage and there are options for you to work at the level of homework that best suits you in your season of life and stage of studying the Word. We believe that your time in the Word each day is vital, but it is between you and the Lord. We are just here to help provide tools and resources for your personal study time each day, and as a guide when we gather each week for class discussions and live teaching on the passage. The Dig In Worksheets are tools to help you inductively study the Bible using sound principles and teach you how to study the Word for yourself and avoid misinterpretation and misapplication.

Our Study

"O Lord, how long...?" At some point in our lives, we can all identify with the prophet Habakkuk's cry to the Lord as he wrestles with God over the suffering and injustice he sees in the world around him. In this 4-week study of Habakkuk, we will learn how to study a book of Old Testament prophecy and discover how to wait, hope, trust, and rejoice in the Lord in the face of life's difficulties and hardships.

Rejoicing in Christ Jesus,

Susan Cady

DIG IN BIBLE STUDY: 6 STEPS TO STUDY THE BIBLE

PRAYER

Get Your Bearings

- Begin with prayer!
- Where does this passage fall in the timeline of the story of the Bible?
- What is the genre of the book? (narrative, poetry, epistle/letter, prophetic)
- Read the passage repeatedly.

OBSERVATION

APPLICATION

"Them/Then"

- What can we observe about the original audience and their time?
- What is happening historically and culturally at the time? Observe the text for clues. Use Bible dictionaries or Bible encyclopedias for more info.
- What is the meaning of the passage to the original audience?
- Make observations on the content and context of the text.
- Note the surrounding context (verses before and after, chapters before and after, and the book as a whole)

"Us/Now"

- Pray! How should I live out this timeless truth today?
- Do I really believe what I have read about who God is? If so, how does that change how I view God, myself, others, and the world?
- Pray! Is there anything I want to change in my life because of this truth?
- Pray! What action will I take today?

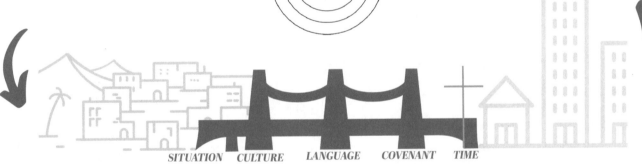

SITUATION   CULTURE   LANGUAGE   COVENANT   TIME

Author's Aim

- What was the author's message to the original audience?
- What are repeated ideas or themes in the passage?
- Summarize the main idea of the passage.
- Write out the author's aim in one or two sentences using past tense verbs.

INTERPRETATION

Timeless Truth

- What is the timeless truth reflected in this text?
- How does the gospel impact the author's original message of the text?
- Consult the biblical map (cross-references) for other places this truth is taught.

Bridge the Gap

- What are the differences and similarities between the original audience and us?
- Look at the situation/circumstances, culture, language, time, and covenant.
- What parts of the text apply only to the biblical audience?

DIG IN BIBLE STUDY: 6 STEPS TO STUDY THE BIBLE

#1 — Get Your Bearings

- Begin with prayer!
- Where does this passage fall in the timeline of the story of the Bible? (Old or New Testament, time period in Israel's history, before or after the cross, etc.)
- What is the genre of the book? (narrative, poetry, epistle/letter, prophetic)
- Read the passage repeatedly.

#2 — "Them/Then"

- What can we observe about the original audience and their time?
- What is happening historically and culturally at the time? Observe the text for clues. Use Bible dictionaries or Bible encyclopedias for more info.
- Make observations on the content and context of the text.
- What are the repeated ideas or themes in the passage?
- Note the surrounding context (verses before and after, chapters before and after, and the book as a whole).
- What is the meaning of the passage to the original audience?

#3 — Author's Aim

- What was the author's message to the original audience?
- Summarize the main idea of the passage.
- Write out the author's aim in one or two sentences using past tense verbs.

#4 — Bridge the Gap

- What are the differences and similarities between the original audience and us?
- Look at the situation/circumstances, culture, language, time, and covenant.
- What parts of the text apply only to the biblical audience?

#5 — Timeless Truth/Gospel Impact

- What is the timeless truth reflected in this text?
- How does the gospel impact the author's original message of the text?
- Consult the biblical map. Look up cross-references for other places in the Bible this truth is taught.

#6 — "Us/Now"

- Pray! How should I live out this timeless truth today?
- Do I really believe what I have read about who God is? If so, how does that change how I view God, myself, others, and the world?
- Is there anything I want to change in my life because of this truth?
- What action will I take today?

WEEK 1

INTRODUCTION

STRUCTURE OF THE BIBLE

5-12-5-5-12

The 39 books of the Old Testament are categorized into five groups.

Pentateuch 5 books	History 12 books	Poetry 5 books	Major Prophets 5 books	Minor Prophets 12 books

Chronologically, the (5) books of poetry, (5) major prophets and (12) minor prophets fit into the (12) books of history.

_____ (5)	_____ (12)	_____ (5)	_____ (5)	_____ (12)
Genesis	Joshua	Job	Isaiah	Hosea
Exodus	Judges	Psalms	Jeremiah	Joel
Leviticus	Ruth	Proverbs	Ezekiel	Amos
Numbers	1 Samuel	Ecclesiastes	Daniel	Obadiah
Deuteronomy	2 Samuel	Song of Solomon	Lamentations	Jonah
	1 Kings			Micah
	2 Kings			Nahum
	1 Chronicles			Habakkuk
	2 Chronicles			Zephaniah
	Ezra			Haggai
	Nehemiah			Zechariah
	Esther			Malachi

4-1-21-1

The 27 books of the Old Testament are categorized into four groups.

Gospels 4 books	History 1 book	Letters/Epistles 21	Prophecy 1 book

_____ (4)	_____ (1)	_____ (21)	_____ (1)
Matthew	Acts	Romans	Revelation
Mark		1 Corinthians	
Luke		2 Corinthians	
John		Galatians	
		Ephesians	
		Philippians	
		Colossians	
		1 Thessalonians	
		2Thessalonians	
		1 Timothy	
		2 Timothy	
		Titus	
		Philemon	
		Hebrews	
		James	
		1 Peter	
		2 Peter	
		1 John	
		2 John	
		3 John	
		Jude	

TIMELINE OF THE BIBLE

CREATION

ABRAHAM (2165-1990 BC)
ISAAC (2065-1885 BC)
JACOB (2000-1860 BC)
JOSEPH (1910-1800 BC)

MOSES (1525-1405 BC)

THE EXODUS & THE LAW (1450 BC)
JOSHUA
THE PROMISED LAND
THE JUDGES (1380-1050 BC)

SAUL (REIGN 1050-1010 BC)
DAVID (REIGN 1010-970 BC)
SOLOMON (REIGN 970-930 BC)

THE TEMPLE (966 BC)

**DIVIDED KINGDOM
(922 BC)**

SOUTHERN KINGDOM: JUDAH
REHOBOAM (REIGN 930-913 BC)

NORTHERN KINGDOM: ISRAEL
JEROBOAM (REIGN 930-909 BC)

ELIJAH (875-848 BC)

ISAIAH (740-681 BC)
MICAH (750-686 BC)

JONAH (786-746 BC)

ZEPHANIAH (640-609 BC)
JEREMIAH (626-585 BC)
HABAKKUK (605-586 BC)

AMOS & HOSEA (745-612 BC)

**SOUTHERN KINGDOM OF JUDAH
EXILED TO BABYLON (586 BC)**

**NORTHERN KINGDOM OF ISRAEL
EXILED TO ASSYRIA (722 BC)**

EZEKIEL
(593-571 BC)

DANIEL
(605-530 BC)

EXILE TO BABYLON (597- 432 BC)

1ST DEPORTATION
(597 BC)

JERUSALEM DESTROYED

2ND DEPORTATION
(586 BC)

OBADIAH (585 BC)

1ST RETURN (538 BC)
under Zerubbabel

ZECHARIAH & HAGGAI (520-480 BC)

2ND RETURN (458 BC)
under Ezra // PERSIAN RULE

LAST RETURN (432 BC)
under Nehemiah // PERSIAN RULE

MALACHI (440-430 BC)

OTHER OT PROPHETS
JOEL TO JUDAH & ISRAEL (722-586 (BC)
NAHUM TO NINEVAH (663-612 BC)

END OF OLD TESTAMENT PERIOD

BETWEEN THE TESTAMENTS (432 BC-5 AD) GREEKS RULE

START OF NEW TESTAMENT PERIOD ROMAN RULE

JESUS BORN (5 BC)   JOHN THE BAPTIST
JESUS BEGINS PUBLIC MINISTRY (26 AD)
JESUS' DEATH, RESURRECTION + ASCENSION (30 AD)
PENTECOST (30 AD)
PAUL CONVERTED (35 AD)
1ST MISSIONARY JOURNEY (46-48 AD)   JAMES MARTYRED + PETER IMPRISONED (44 AD)
2ND MISSIONARY JOURNEY (50-52 AD)   JERUSALEM COUNSEL (49-50 AD)
3RD MISSIONARY JOURNEY (53-57 AD)
PAUL IMPRISONED IN ROME (59-61 AD)
END OF NEW TESTAMENT PERIOD   JOHN EXILED ON PATMOS (90-95 AD)
"ALREADY, BUT NOT YET" // AWAITING CHRIST'S RETURN

OLD TESTAMENT PROPHETS & THEIR AUDIENCE

Prophet	Audience	King(s)	Approx. Date(s)
Isaiah	To Judah (South)	Uzziah, Jotham, Ahaz, Hezekiah, Manasseh	760-673 BC
Jeremiah	To Judah (South)	Manasseh, Amon, Josiah, Jehoahaz, Jehoiakim, Jehoiachin, Zedekiah	650-582 BC
Ezekiel	To Exiles in Babylon	Josiah, Jehoahaz, Jehoiakim, Jehoiachin, Zedekiah	620-570 BC
Daniel	To Exiles in Babylon	Josiah, Jehoahaz, Jehoiakim, Jehoiachin, Zedekiah	620-540 BC
Hosea	To Israel (North)	Jeroboam II, Zechariah, Shallum, Menahem, Pekahiah, Pekah, Hoshea	758-725 BC
Joel	To Judah (South)	Govenor Ezra	450 BC
Amos	To Israel (North)	Jeroboam II	765-754 BC
Obadiah	Concerning Edom	Zedekiah	590 BC
Jonah	To Ninevah	Jeroboam II	781 BC
Micah	To Judah (South)	Jotham, Ahaz, Hezekiah, Manasseh	738-698 BC
Nahum	Concerning Ninevah	Manasseh, Amon, Josiah	658-615 BC
Habakkuk	To Judah (South)	Jehoiakim, Jehoiachin	608-598 BC
Zephaniah	To Judah (South)	Amon, Josiah	640-626 BC
Haggai	To Judah (Persian Period)	Governor Zerubbabel	520 BC
Zechariah	To Judah (Persian Period)	Governor Zerubbabel	522-509 BC
Malachi	To Judah (Persian Period)	Governor Zerubbabel	465 BC

INTRODUCTION

BOOKS

Isaiah, Jeremiah, Lamentations, Ezekiel, Daniel, Hosea, Joel, Amos, Obadiah, Jonah, Micah, Nahum, Habakkuk, Zephaniah, Haggai, Zechariah, Malachi

GENRE/STYLE

CHRONOLOGICAL ORDER: In the Old Testament, the books of the prophets are chronologically arranged within the historical accounts of 1 Samuel through Nehemiah. This order helps us understand the development of prophetic literature and its historical context. The prophetic books primarily consist of short-spoken or preached messages, usually delivered by the prophet to either the nation of Israel or the nation of Judah. They also contain visions from God, short narrative sections, and symbolic acts.

PROPHECY: Only a small percentage of the prophecy in these books refers to events that are future to us. **"Less than two percent of Old Testament prophecy is messianic. Less than five percent specifically describes the new covenant age. Less than one percent concerns events yet to come in our time."** (Duvall & Hays, 2007) Most of the prophecy in these books addresses the disobedience of the nation of Israel and/or Judah and their impending judgment.

STYLE: The prophet-writers employ poetry as their primary tool, using extensive figurative language to convey their messages. These figures of speech, far from being mere embellishments, are powerful weapons that drive home their point and God's message to His people. For instance, instead of simply stating, "God is angry," the prophet Amos uses a vivid metaphor, proclaiming, "The lion has roared" (Amos 3:8). This use of figurative language adds a layer of intrigue and fascination to the prophetic literature, making it a compelling and thought-provoking read. The texts also feature narratives, oracles, and visions, adding further layers of depth to the oral message units.

MESSAGE OF THE PROPHETS

The prophets were covenant enforcement mediators. The prophets were God's direct representatives and their message was not their own, but God's. The prophets' message is not original. Very little, if anything, is truly new in the way of commands.

The prophet's basic message was a call to repentance because the Israelites had broken the covenant. There are three basic indictments:
- idolatry
- social injustice
- religious ritualism

If the Israelites refused to repent, then judgment would come, yet there was hope beyond judgment for a future restoration.

A WORD OF CAUTION: THE PROPHET AS FORETELLER OF THE FUTURE

The prophets did indeed predict the future, but that future is mostly our past. Some prophecies of the prophets' near future were set against the background of the great eschatological future. The Bible regularly sees God's acts in temporal history in light of his overall plan for humanity.

TIMELINE OF THE PROPHETIC BOOKS

The books of the prophets were written during the time when Israel was a divided kingdom: North/Israel and South/Judah. The prophets all correspond to the historical narratives of 1-2 Kings and 1-2 Chronicles, so it is important to read these corresponding passages. Although the specific situations and culture may differ from ours, the messages are extremely relevant to our own times and history.

All 16 of the prophetic books were from the period of around 760–460 BC—a relatively short period of time in the scope of biblical history.

There are three time periods of Israel/Judah's history when the prophetic books were written. the prophets can be classified as pre-exilic, post-exilic and

There are three important points to remember when studying the books of the prophets regarding the period in the nation of Israel's history.

1. There is significant political, military, economic, and social upheaval.
2. There is a very high level of unfaithfulness and disregard for the Mosaic covenant.
3. There are enormous shifts in the balance of power internationally.

LITERARY & HISTORICAL CONTEXT FOR THE PROPHETIC BOOKS

LITERARY

In the prophets, we "think oracles" rather than paragraphs. Understanding where an oracle begins and ends can make a big difference in how one understands the setting.

The Forms of Prophetic Utterance
The five most common forms are:
- The lawsuit (Isaiah 3:13–26)
- The woe (Habakkuk 2:6–8)
- The promise (Amos 9:11–15)
- The enactment prophecy (Isaiah 20)
- The messenger speech (Malachi 1:2–5)

HISTORICAL

When studying the prophetic books, it is necessary to keep in mind the larger context (prophetic era) and the specific context (that of a single oracle).

Because of historical distance, it is a clear necessity that we seek secondary help in order to understand the context and what is being said. Bible dictionaries and handbooks can be very helpful for these purposes.

STRUCTURE OF HABAKKUK

Here are a few things to look for as you read Habakkuk:

Habakkuk is unique from the other books of the major and minor prophets in two ways. First, the prophet does not address the nation of Israel but converses with God. Second, the prophet himself undergoes a spiritual transformation.

The first two chapters of the book follow the format of a drama with a **question-and-answer pattern**. There is also a **rhetorical pattern of pairing two-plus-one**: The prophet complains twice, listens to God twice, and prays once.

Habakkuk comprises two compositions of different literary genres: an oracle and a poem/psalm with a common theme.

In Habakkuk, we find an **oracle of judgment**. An oracle of judgment contains a description of the corruptness of evil societies and a prediction that God will punish those societies through military defeat.

Habakkuk contains a **woe formula**. One common form of oracles of judgment is the pronouncement of coming calamity. The woe formula is a standard format for these predictions, with the pronouncement beginning with "woe to…"

Typically, a woe formula is followed by **oracles of salvation and blessing**. Instead, in Habakkuk, we find a **parody**. A parody is when a writer imitates an existing genre but with a striking twist. In Habakkuk, instead of oracles of salvation and blessing, we find a **theophany** followed by a personal testimony. A theophany is an earthly appearance of the transcendent God. Commonly, the imagery of nature is used to convey how the observer perceives the presence of God.

Habakkuk was a poet and a prophet, and in chapter 3, we find an **exalted lyric poem or psalm**.

BACKGROUND OF HABAKKUK

Habakkuk is a pre-exilic book in the 6th century B.C. (approx. 607), and the prophet was a contemporary of Jeremiah. Habakkuk was a prophet to Judah (Southern Kingdom). The message of the pre-exilic prophets was a message of hope despite impending judgment. Despite the judgment that God was preparing to bring through the Assyrians and Babylonians it was within the context of God's great acts for Israel in the past that become the hope for God's restoration of Israel in the future. Habakkuk and Jeremiah introduced the concept of personal religion versus corporate religion of the nation(s) of Israel/Judah. Several prophets used theodicy, a defense of God's power and goodness in a world in which evil exists; an explanation for why God allows bad things to happen to people. These prophets include Isaiah, Nahum, Habakkuk, and Job is a good example even though he is not a prophet.

DIG IN BIBLE STUDY WORKSHEET

SCRIPTURE PASSAGE: <u>2 Kings 22-23; 2 Chronicles 34:1-36:4</u>

BACKGROUND OF HABAKKUK

KEYWORD/TERMS/PHRASES:

STEP 1: GET YOUR BEARINGS

PRAY!

Genre: _____ Testament: _____

Where does this passage fall in the timeline of Scripture?

_____

Author: _____

STEP 2: "THEM/THEN"

CONTEXT (HISTORICAL/CULTURAL) What does the text reveal about the historical or cultural situation?

2 Kings 22-23 and 2 Chronicles 34:1-36:4 provide the historical background for the book of Habakkuk. What can you glean from these passages regarding the time period and situation for the original audience of the book?

Consider the following questions:
- Who was the author? What was his background? When did he write?
- Who was the biblical audience, including their culture and social customs?
- What were their circumstances, including the social or political situation?
- Are there any other historical-cultural factors that might shed light on the passage/book?

GOD IS...

Whenever you read a verse or passage of Scripture, look for what you learn about who God is—His names, attributes, ways and works. Building a storehouse in your heart and mind of who God is, will serve as an anchor for your soul in suffering.

2 Kings 22-23; 2 Chronicles 34:1-36:4

_____

_____

_____

_____

_____

_____

_____

_____

_____

_____

_____

_____

_____

_____

_____

Repetition of Words/Phrases (Examples in 2 Corinthians 1:3-7, John 15:1-10, 1 Corinthians 15:50-54)
Look for words or phrases that repeat. How many times is it repeated in the verses you are studying? Is this word or term repeated in the surrounding context? Does the repeated word always serve the same function? Does the repeated word/phrase have the same meaning each time it occurs?

Contrasts (Examples in Proverbs 15:1, Romans 6:23, Ephesians 5:8, 1 John 1: 5-7)
Look for contrasts. Contrasts focus on differences. What word signals the contrast? What ideas, individuals, or items are being contrasted?
Common Signal Words for Contrast: *although, besides, but, compared with, even though, furthermore, more than, otherwise, rather than, though, unless, unlike, while, yet*

Comparisons (Examples in James 3:3-6, Isaiah 40:31)
Look for comparisons. Comparisons focus on similarities. What word signals the comparison? What ideas, individuals, or items are being compared?
Common Signal Words for Comparison: *also, as well as, both, in the same way, in addition, just as, like, similarly, the same as, too*

Lists (Example in 1 John 2:16)
When you see more than two itemized things, you are observing a list. How many items are in the list? What items are in the list? Is there any significance to how the items are grouped?

Cause and Effect (Examples in Psalm 13:6, John 3:16, Colossians 3:1)
Look for cause-and-effect relationships. Does the cause have one effect or more than one? What is the cause and effect you note in the sentence?

Conjunctions (Examples in Romans 6:23, Hebrews 12:1, Colossians 3:12, 2 Timothy 1:7-8)
Conjunctions hold our phrases and sentences together. What function does the conjunction serve—connecting (and), contrasting (but), or concluding (therefore)?
Common Signal Words for Conjunctions: *and, for, but, therefore, since, because*

Verbs (Examples in Ephesians 4:2-3, Colossians 3:1, Ephesians 1:11, Genesis 12:3)
Verbs communicate the action of the sentence. List the verbs in the verse. Identify the tense of the verb: past, present, future, etc. What is the "voice" of the verb: active or passive? Is the verb an imperative (a command)? Who is the subject of the verb?

Figures of Speech (Examples in Psalm 119:105, Matthew 23:27)
Figures of speech are when images are communicated with words used in a sense other than the normal, literal sense. Visualize the image that is communicated in the sentence(s).

Pronouns (Example in Philippians 1:27-30)
Pronouns take the place of nouns. Identify the pronouns and the noun they replace.

"BIG 6" QUESTIONS: WHO, WHAT, WHERE, WHEN, WHY & HOW
- Who are the people in the text?
- What is happening in the text?
- What are the events taking place?
- What is the point being made?
- When did the events in the passage take place?
- Where is this taking place?
- How did this occur? How are people/places connected?
- Why is this included? Why does this person say that? Why is this important?

STEP 2: "THEM/THEN"

CONTEXT (LITERARY)   Using the Sentence Observations List and "Big 6" Questions, note your observations.

_____

_____

_____

_____

_____

_____

_____

_____

_____

_____

_____

_____

_____

_____

_____

_____

_____

_____

_____

_____

_____

_____

STEP 2: "THEM/THEN"

CONTEXT (LITERARY)   After making observations on the text, answer the questions below.

What has happened so far in the narrative? Have there been any major events, characters or themes?

What has happened just before the section you are reading?

What do you learn about the main characters in this section? How does the author describe them? How do they describe themselves?

Is time or place significant in the events that happen in the passage?

Is there a conflict or high point in the passage?

Do you find anything surprising or confusing in the passage?

STEP 3: AUTHOR'S AIM

Answer the following questions to help determine the author's intended meaning of the passage for the original audience.

Do you think there is a main point or theme in this section of the story?

Are there any comments from the author about the events in the narrative? How do these comments shed light on what is happening?

Does someone in the narrative learn something or grow in some way? How? What does this person learn?

STEP 3: AUTHOR'S AIM

Summarize the message of the passage for the original audience in a few sentences using past tense verbs.

_____

_____

_____

_____

_____

STEP 4: BRIDGE THE GAP

Compare the biblical audience and their time with our time and culture today. Note any differences in language or terms used, in the situation, in the culture, and in the covenant (Old or New).

"Them/Then"	"Us/Now"

What parts of the text apply only to the biblical audience?

_____

_____

_____

_____

_____

STEP 5: TIMELESS TRUTH/PRINCIPLE(S)

(Timeless truth is a principle that applies to all people across time. It should relate to your Author's Aim of the passage and consider the differences/similarities in Step 4. State the timeless truth in a sentence or two using present tense verbs. Consider how the Gospel impacts this truth.)

_____

_____

_____

_____

STEP 5: CONSULT THE BIBLICAL MAP

- Do the principles/truths you noted fit with the rest of Scripture?
- Use cross-references to determine other places this truth or principle is used in the Bible.

STEP 6: "US/NOW" (APPLICATION)

- What have I learned about who God is? Do I really believe what I have learned about who God is? If so, how does that change the way I view God, myself, others, and the world?
- Does how I think about God day to day fit with the picture of Him that I have just studied?
- Is there anything I want to change in my life in view of this? What action will I take today?

_____

_____

_____

_____

_____

_____

_____

"WHY, O LORD, DO YOU STAND FAR AWAY? WHY DO YOU HIDE YOURSELF IN TIMES OF TROUBLE?"
—PSALM 10:1

"HOW LONG, O LORD? WILL YOU FORGET ME FOREVER? HOW LONG WILL YOU HIDE YOUR FACE FROM ME?
—PSALM 13:1

HOMEWORK

Habakkuk 1:1:-2:1

GOD IS...

Whenever you read a verse or passage of Scripture, look for what you learn about who God is—His names, attributes, ways and works. Building a storehouse in your heart and mind of who God is, will serve as an anchor for your soul in suffering.

Habakkuk 1:1-2:1

_____

_____

_____

_____

_____

_____

_____

_____

_____

_____

_____

_____

_____

_____

_____

_____

DIG IN BIBLE STUDY WORKSHEET

SCRIPTURE PASSAGE: _____Habakkuk 1:1-2:1_____

KEYWORD/TERMS/PHRASES:

STEP 1: GET YOUR BEARINGS

PRAY!

Genre: _____ Testament: _____

Where does this passage fall in the timeline of Scripture?

_____

Author: _____

STEP 2: "THEM/THEN"

CONTEXT (HISTORICAL/CULTURAL) What does the text reveal about the historical or cultural situation?

Consider the following questions:
- Who was the author? What was his background?
- When did he write?
- Who was the biblical audience, including their culture and social customs?
- What were their circumstances, including the social or political situation?
- What was happening in the audience's world when the book was written?
- Are there any other historical-cultural factors that might shed light on the passage/book?

LITERARY OBSERVATIONS SHEET

Repetition of Words/Phrases (Examples in 2 Corinthians 1:3-7, John 15:1-10, 1 Corinthians 15:50-54)
Look for words or phrases that repeat. How many times is it repeated in the verses you are studying? Is this word or term repeated in the surrounding context? Does the repeated word always serve the same function? Does the repeated word/phrase have the same meaning each time it occurs?

Contrasts (Examples in Proverbs 15:1, Romans 6:23, Ephesians 5:8, 1 John 1: 5-7)
Look for contrasts. Contrasts focus on differences. What word signals the contrast? What ideas, individuals, or items are being contrasted?
Common Signal Words for Contrast: *although, besides, but, compared with, even though, furthermore, more than, otherwise, rather than, though, unless, unlike, while, yet*

Comparisons (Examples in James 3:3-6, Isaiah 40:31)
Look for comparisons. Comparisons focus on similarities. What word signals the comparison? What ideas, individuals, or items are being compared?
Common Signal Words for Comparison: *also, as well as, both, in the same way, in addition, just as, like, similarly, the same as, too*

Lists (Example in 1 John 2:16)
When you see more than two itemized things, you are observing a list. How many items are in the list? What items are in the list? Is there any significance to how the items are grouped?

Cause and Effect (Examples in Psalm 13:6, John 3:16, Colossians 3:1)
Look for cause-and-effect relationships. Does the cause have one effect or more than one? What is the cause and effect you note in the sentence?

Conjunctions (Examples in Romans 6:23, Hebrews 12:1, Colossians 3:12, 2 Timothy 1:7-8)
Conjunctions hold our phrases and sentences together. What function does the conjunction serve—connecting (and), contrasting (but), or concluding (therefore)?
Common Signal Words for Conjunctions: *and, for, but, therefore, since, because*

Verbs (Examples in Ephesians 4:2-3, Colossians 3:1, Ephesians 1:11, Genesis 12:3)
Verbs communicate the action of the sentence. List the verbs in the verse. Identify the tense of the verb: past, present, future, etc. What is the "voice" of the verb: active or passive? Is the verb an imperative (a command)? Who is the subject of the verb?

Figures of Speech (Examples in Psalm 119:105, Matthew 23:27)
Figures of speech are when images are communicated with words used in a sense other than the normal, literal sense. Visualize the image that is communicated in the sentence(s).

Pronouns (Example in Philippians 1:27-30)
Pronouns take the place of nouns. Identify the pronouns and the noun they replace.

"BIG 6" QUESTIONS: WHO, WHAT, WHERE, WHEN, WHY & HOW

- Who are the people in the text?
- What is happening in the text?
- What are the events taking place?
- What is the point being made?
- When did the events in the passage take place?
- Where is this taking place?
- How did this occur? How are people/places connected?
- Why is this included? Why does this person say that? Why is this important?

STEP 2: "THEM/THEN"

CONTEXT (LITERARY) Using the Sentence Observations List and "Big 6" Questions, note your observations.

_____

_____

_____

_____

_____

_____

_____

_____

_____

_____

_____

_____

_____

_____

_____

_____

_____

_____

_____

_____

_____

_____

_____

STEP 2: "THEM/THEN"

CONTEXT (LITERARY)   After making observations on the text, answer the questions below.

Are there any clues about the circumstances in which the prophecy was given or written?

Are there any people or places mentioned that you aren't familiar with? (Look them up in earlier parts of the book, or refer to a Bible dictionary, Bible atlas, or Bible encyclopedia)

Are other parts of the Old Testament mentioned or alluded to in the passage? What part do these 'memories' play in the text?

Are there any repetitions or multiple instances of similar ideas? Do these repetitions make a particular point or point to the structure of the passage?

Paying attention to when the prophet is speaking and when God is speaking, what does the passage tell us about God's plans? What does it tell us about God's character?

STEP 3: AUTHOR'S AIM

Answer the following questions to help determine the author's intended meaning of the passage for the original audience.

What is the main point or points?

Are there any specific instructions/commands given to the reader?

Does this passage mention any consequences for not following God's commands?

What kind of behavior, if any, is condemned or rewarded? What response is called for, if any?

Does the text have a sense of expectation about something happening in the future? What is to be expected and when? Does it motivate any action?

Does the passage point forward to Jesus, or is the gospel anticipated/foreshadowed?

STEP 3: AUTHOR'S AIM

Summarize the message of the passage for the original audience in a few sentences using past tense verbs.

_____

_____

_____

_____

_____

STEP 4: BRIDGE THE GAP

Compare the biblical audience and their time with our time and culture today. Note any differences in language or terms used, in the situation, in the culture, and in the covenant (Old or New).

"Them/Then"	"Us/Now"

What parts of the text apply only to the biblical audience?

_____

_____

_____

_____

_____

_____

STEP 5: TIMELESS TRUTH/PRINCIPLE(S)

(Timeless truth is a principle that applies to all people across time. It should relate to your Author's Aim of the passage and consider the differences/similarities in Step 4. State the timeless truth in a sentence or two using present tense verbs. Consider how the Gospel impacts this truth.)

_____

_____

_____

_____

STEP 5: CONSULT THE BIBLICAL MAP

- Do the principles/truths you noted fit with the rest of Scripture?
- Use cross-references to determine other places this truth or principle is used in the Bible.

STEP 6: "US/NOW" (APPLICATION)

- What have I learned about who God is? Do I really believe what I have learned about who God is? If so, how does that change the way I view God, myself, others, and the world?
- Does how I think about God day to day fit with the picture of Him that I have just studied?
- Is there anything I want to change in my life in view of this? What action will I take today?

_____

_____

_____

_____

_____

_____

_____

O LORD,
HOW LONG
SHALL I CRY
FOR HELP, AND
YOU WILL NOT
HEAR?

—HABAKKUK 1:2

WEEK 2

Habakkuk 1:1:-2:1

HOMEWORK

Habakkuk 2:2-20

GOD IS...

Whenever you read a verse or passage of Scripture, look for what you learn about who God is—His names, attributes, ways and works. Building a storehouse in your heart and mind of who God is, will serve as an anchor for your soul in suffering.

Habakkuk 1:1-2:1

_____
_____
_____
_____
_____
_____
_____
_____
_____
_____
_____
_____
_____
_____
_____
_____
_____
_____

DIG IN BIBLE STUDY WORKSHEET

SCRIPTURE PASSAGE: ___Habakkuk 2:2-20___

KEYWORD/TERMS/PHRASES:

STEP 1: GET YOUR BEARINGS

PRAY!

Genre: _____ Testament: _____

Where does this passage fall in the timeline of Scripture?

_____

Author: _____

STEP 2: "THEM/THEN"

CONTEXT (HISTORICAL/CULTURAL) What does the text reveal about the historical or cultural situation?

Consider the following questions:
- o Who was the author? What was his background?
- o When did he write?
- o Who was the biblical audience, including their culture and social customs?
- o What were their circumstances, including the social or political situation?
- o What was happening in the audience's world when the book was written?
- o Are there any other historical-cultural factors that might shed light on the passage/book?

_____

_____

_____

_____

_____

_____

_____

_____

_____

_____

Repetition of Words/Phrases (Examples in 2 Corinthians 1:3-7, John 15:1-10, 1 Corinthians 15:50-54)
Look for words or phrases that repeat. How many times is it repeated in the verses you are studying? Is this word or term repeated in the surrounding context? Does the repeated word always serve the same function? Does the repeated word/phrase have the same meaning each time it occurs?

Contrasts (Examples in Proverbs 15:1, Romans 6:23, Ephesians 5:8, 1 John 1: 5-7)
Look for contrasts. Contrasts focus on differences. What word signals the contrast? What ideas, individuals, or items are being contrasted?
Common Signal Words for Contrast: *although, besides, but, compared with, even though, furthermore, more than, otherwise, rather than, though, unless, unlike, while, yet*

Comparisons (Examples in James 3:3-6, Isaiah 40:31)
Look for comparisons. Comparisons focus on similarities. What word signals the comparison? What ideas, individuals, or items are being compared?
Common Signal Words for Comparison: *also, as well as, both, in the same way, in addition, just as, like, similarly, the same as, too*

Lists (Example in 1 John 2:16)
When you see more than two itemized things, you are observing a list. How many items are in the list? What items are in the list? Is there any significance to how the items are grouped?

Cause and Effect (Examples in Psalm 13:6, John 3:16, Colossians 3:1)
Look for cause-and-effect relationships. Does the cause have one effect or more than one? What is the cause and effect you note in the sentence?

Conjunctions (Examples in Romans 6:23, Hebrews 12:1, Colossians 3:12, 2 Timothy 1:7-8)
Conjunctions hold our phrases and sentences together. What function does the conjunction serve—connecting (and), contrasting (but), or concluding (therefore)?
Common Signal Words for Conjunctions: *and, for, but, therefore, since, because*

Verbs (Examples in Ephesians 4:2-3, Colossians 3:1, Ephesians 1:11, Genesis 12:3)
Verbs communicate the action of the sentence. List the verbs in the verse. Identify the tense of the verb: past, present, future, etc. What is the "voice" of the verb: active or passive? Is the verb an imperative (a command)? Who is the subject of the verb?

Figures of Speech (Examples in Psalm 119:105, Matthew 23:27)
Figures of speech are when images are communicated with words used in a sense other than the normal, literal sense. Visualize the image that is communicated in the sentence(s).

Pronouns (Example in Philippians 1:27-30)
Pronouns take the place of nouns. Identify the pronouns and the noun they replace.

"BIG 6" QUESTIONS: WHO, WHAT, WHERE, WHEN, WHY & HOW

- Who are the people in the text?
- What is happening in the text?
- What are the events taking place?
- What is the point being made?
- When did the events in the passage take place?
- Where is this taking place?
- How did this occur? How are people/places connected?
- Why is this included? Why does this person say that? Why is this important?

STEP 2: "THEM/THEN"

CONTEXT (LITERARY)   Using the Sentence Observations List and "Big 6" Questions, note your observations.

_____

_____

_____

_____

_____

_____

_____

_____

_____

_____

_____

_____

_____

_____

_____

_____

_____

_____

_____

_____

_____

_____

_____

_____

STEP 2: "THEM/THEN"

CONTEXT (LITERARY)   After making observations on the text, answer the questions below.
Are there any clues about the circumstances in which the prophecy was given or written?

Are there any people or places mentioned that you aren't familiar with? (Look them up in earlier parts of the book, or refer to a Bible dictionary, Bible atlas, or Bible encyclopedia)

Are other parts of the Old Testament mentioned or alluded to in the passage? What part do these 'memories' play in the text?

Are there any repetitions or multiple instances of similar ideas? Do these repetitions make a particular point or point to the structure of the passage?

Paying attention to when the prophet is speaking and when God is speaking, what does the passage tell us about God's plans? What does it tell us about God's character?

STEP 3: AUTHOR'S AIM

Answer the following questions to help determine the author's intended meaning of the passage for the original audience.

What is the main point or points?

Are there any specific instructions/commands given to the reader?

Does this passage mention any consequences for not following God's commands?

What kind of behavior, if any, is condemned or rewarded? What response is called for, if any?

Does the text have a sense of expectation about something happening in the future? What is to be expected and when? Does it motivate any action?

Does the passage point forward to Jesus, or is the gospel anticipated/foreshadowed?

STEP 3: AUTHOR'S AIM

Summarize the message of the passage for the original audience in a few sentences using past tense verbs.

_____

_____

_____

_____

_____

STEP 4: BRIDGE THE GAP

Compare the biblical audience and their time with our time and culture today. Note any differences in language or terms used, in the situation, in the culture, and in the covenant (Old or New).

"Them/Then"	"Us/Now"

What parts of the text apply only to the biblical audience?

_____

_____

_____

_____

_____

_____

STEP 5: TIMELESS TRUTH/PRINCIPLE(S)

(Timeless truth is a principle that applies to all people across time. It should relate to your Author's Aim of the passage and consider the differences/similarities in Step 4. State the timeless truth in a sentence or two using present tense verbs. Consider how the Gospel impacts this truth.)

_____

_____

_____

_____

STEP 5: CONSULT THE BIBLICAL MAP

- Do the principles/truths you noted fit with the rest of Scripture?
- Use cross-references to determine other places this truth or principle is used in the Bible.

STEP 6: "US/NOW" (APPLICATION)

- What have I learned about who God is? Do I really believe what I have learned about who God is? If so, how does that change the way I view God, myself, others, and the world?
- Does how I think about God day to day fit with the picture of Him that I have just studied?
- Is there anything I want to change in my life in view of this? What action will I take today?

_____

_____

_____

_____

_____

_____

_____

"FOR STILL THE VISION AWAITS ITS APPOINTED TIME; IT HASTENS TO THE END — IT WILL NOT LIE. IF IT SEEMS SLOW, WAIT FOR IT; IT WILL SURELY COME; IT WILL NOT DELAY.

—HABAKKUK 2:3

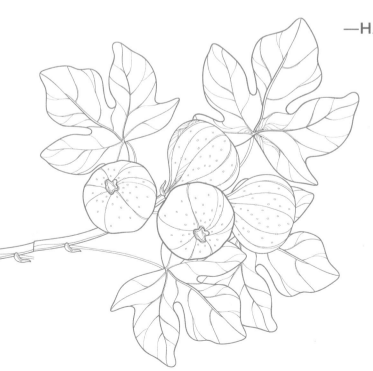

WEEK 3

Habakkuk 2:2-20

WOE	IMAGERY

HOMEWORK

Habakkuk 3:1-19

GOD IS...

Whenever you read a verse or passage of Scripture, look for what you learn about who God is—His names, attributes, ways and works. Building a storehouse in your heart and mind of who God is, will serve as an anchor for your soul in suffering.

Habakkuk 1:1-2:1

DIG IN BIBLE STUDY WORKSHEET

SCRIPTURE PASSAGE: ___Habakkuk 3:1-19___

KEYWORD/TERMS/PHRASES:

STEP 1: GET YOUR BEARINGS

PRAY!

Genre: _____ Testament: _____

Where does this passage fall in the timeline of Scripture?

_____

Author: _____

STEP 2: "THEM/THEN"

CONTEXT (HISTORICAL/CULTURAL) What does the text reveal about the historical or cultural situation?

Consider the following questions:
- Who was the author? What was his background?
- When did he write?
- Who was the biblical audience, including their culture and social customs?
- What were their circumstances, including the social or political situation?
- What was happening in the audience's world when the book was written?
- Are there any other historical-cultural factors that might shed light on the passage/book?

Repetition of Words/Phrases (Examples in 2 Corinthians 1:3-7, John 15:1-10, 1 Corinthians 15:50-54)

Look for words or phrases that repeat. How many times is it repeated in the verses you are studying? Is this word or term repeated in the surrounding context? Does the repeated word always serve the same function? Does the repeated word/phrase have the same meaning each time it occurs?

Contrasts (Examples in Proverbs 15:1, Romans 6:23, Ephesians 5:8, 1 John 1: 5-7)

Look for contrasts. Contrasts focus on differences. What word signals the contrast? What ideas, individuals, or items are being contrasted?

Common Signal Words for Contrast: *although, besides, but, compared with, even though, furthermore, more than, otherwise, rather than, though, unless, unlike, while, yet*

Comparisons (Examples in James 3:3-6, Isaiah 40:31)

Look for comparisons. Comparisons focus on similarities. What word signals the comparison? What ideas, individuals, or items are being compared?

Common Signal Words for Comparison: *also, as well as, both, in the same way, in addition, just as, like, similarly, the same as, too*

Lists (Example in 1 John 2:16)

When you see more than two itemized things, you are observing a list. How many items are in the list? What items are in the list? Is there any significance to how the items are grouped?

Cause and Effect (Examples in Psalm 13:6, John 3:16, Colossians 3:1)

Look for cause-and-effect relationships. Does the cause have one effect or more than one? What is the cause and effect you note in the sentence?

Conjunctions (Examples in Romans 6:23, Hebrews 12:1, Colossians 3:12, 2 Timothy 1:7-8)

Conjunctions hold our phrases and sentences together. What function does the conjunction serve—connecting (and), contrasting (but), or concluding (therefore)?

Common Signal Words for Conjunctions: *and, for, but, therefore, since, because*

Verbs (Examples in Ephesians 4:2-3, Colossians 3:1, Ephesians 1:11, Genesis 12:3)

Verbs communicate the action of the sentence. List the verbs in the verse. Identify the tense of the verb: past, present, future, etc. What is the "voice" of the verb: active or passive? Is the verb an imperative (a command)? Who is the subject of the verb?

Figures of Speech (Examples in Psalm 119:105, Matthew 23:27)

Figures of speech are when images are communicated with words used in a sense other than the normal, literal sense. Visualize the image that is communicated in the sentence(s).

Pronouns (Example in Philippians 1:27-30)

Pronouns take the place of nouns. Identify the pronouns and the noun they replace.

"BIG 6" QUESTIONS: WHO, WHAT, WHERE, WHEN, WHY & HOW

- Who are the people in the text?
- What is happening in the text?
- What are the events taking place?
- What is the point being made?
- When did the events in the passage take place?
- Where is this taking place?
- How did this occur? How are people/places connected?
- Why is this included? Why does this person say that? Why is this important?

STEP 2: "THEM/THEN"

CONTEXT (LITERARY)   Using the Sentence Observations List and "Big 6" Questions, note your observations.

_____

_____

_____

_____

_____

_____

_____

_____

_____

_____

_____

_____

_____

_____

_____

_____

_____

_____

_____

_____

_____

_____

STEP 2: "THEM/THEN"

CONTEXT (LITERARY)   After making observations on the text, answer the questions below.

Are there any clues about the circumstances in which the prophecy was given or written?

Are there any people or places mentioned that you aren't familiar with? (Look them up in earlier parts of the book, or refer to a Bible dictionary, Bible atlas, or Bible encyclopedia)

Are other parts of the Old Testament mentioned or alluded to in the passage? What part do these 'memories' play in the text?

Are there any repetitions or multiple instances of similar ideas? Do these repetitions make a particular point or point to the structure of the passage?

Paying attention to when the prophet is speaking and when God is speaking, what does the passage tell us about God's plans? What does it tell us about God's character?

STEP 3: AUTHOR'S AIM

Answer the following questions to help determine the author's intended meaning of the passage for the original audience.

What is the main point or points?

Are there any specific instructions/commands given to the reader?

Does this passage mention any consequences for not following God's commands?

What kind of behavior, if any, is condemned or rewarded? What response is called for, if any?

Does the text have a sense of expectation about something happening in the future? What is to be expected and when? Does it motivate any action?

Does the passage point forward to Jesus, or is the gospel anticipated/foreshadowed?

STEP 3: AUTHOR'S AIM

Summarize the message of the passage for the original audience in a few sentences using past tense verbs.

_____

_____

_____

_____

_____

STEP 4: BRIDGE THE GAP

Compare the biblical audience and their time with our time and culture today. Note any differences in language or terms used, in the situation, in the culture, and in the covenant (Old or New).

"Them/Then"	"Us/Now"

What parts of the text apply only to the biblical audience?

_____

_____

_____

_____

_____

_____

STEP 5: TIMELESS TRUTH/PRINCIPLE(S)

(Timeless truth is a principle that applies to all people across time. It should relate to your Author's Aim of the passage and consider the differences/similarities in Step 4. State the timeless truth in a sentence or two using present tense verbs. Consider how the Gospel impacts this truth.)

_____

_____

_____

_____

STEP 5: CONSULT THE BIBLICAL MAP

- Do the principles/truths you noted fit with the rest of Scripture?
- Use cross-references to determine other places this truth or principle is used in the Bible.

STEP 6: "US/NOW" (APPLICATION)

- What have I learned about who God is? Do I really believe what I have learned about who God is? If so, how does that change the way I view God, myself, others, and the world?
- Does how I think about God day to day fit with the picture of Him that I have just studied?
- Is there anything I want to change in my life in view of this? What action will I take today?

_____

_____

_____

_____

_____

_____

_____

THOUGH THE FIG
TREE SHOULD NOT
BLOSSOM, NOR
FRUIT BE ON THE
VINES, THE
PRODUCE OF THE
OLIVE FAIL AND
THE FIELDS YIELD
NO FOOD...YET I
WILL REJOICE IN
THE LORD;"

—HABAKKUK 3:17-18

WEEK 4

Habakkuk 3:1-19

Additional Resources

Bible Study Resources

The following resources will help determine the historical-cultural context:
- Bible Atlases
- Bible Dictionaries
- Bible Encyclopedias
- Background Commentaries
- Books on ancient life and culture
- Introductions found in your Bible at the beginning of a book

PRINT RESOURCES:
- How to Read the Bible Book by Book - Gordon Fee & Douglas Stuart
- The Baker Illustrated Bible Background Commentary - J.Scott Duvall & J. Daniel Hays
- IVP Bible Background Commentary: Old Testament - John Walton
- IVP Bible Background Commentary: New Testament - Craig Keener

ONLINE RESOURCES:
- **International Standard Bible Encyclopedia:** https://www.biblestudytools.com/encyclopedias/isbe/
- **Bible Commentary:** https://www.studylight.org/commentary.html (The first part has whole Bible commentaries. Scroll down for commentaries on the Old Testament and the New Testament).
- **Holman Bible Dictionary:** https://www.studylight.org/dictionaries/hbd.html
- **Baker's Evangelical Dictionary:** https://www.biblestudytools.com/dictionaries/bakers-evangelical-dictionary/
- **Online Bible Atlas:** https://www.godweb.org/atlasindex.htm
- **Biblical and Cultural Backgrounds:** https://www.lifeintheholyland.com/
- **Bible Atlas:** https://www.openbible.info/geo/atlas/
- **Bible Maps and Charts:** https://www.biblestudy.org/maps/main.html
- **Bible Places:** https://www.bibleplaces.com/
- **Bible Study Tools:** https://www.biblestudytools.com
- **Bible.org:** https://www.bible.org (a comprenhensive Bible study portal)
- **The Bible Project:** https://www.bibleproject.com (great overviews of books of the Bible)
- **Got Questions?:** https://www.gotquestions.org
- **The Gospel Coalition:** https://www.thegospelcoalition.org

APPS (TO BUILD A PERSONAL BIBLE STUDY LIBRARY)
- **Olive Tree Bible software/app** - olivetree.com (free app w/some free resources and then ability to purchase additional resources for library as desired.)
- **Logos Bible software/app** - logos.com (more advanced; cost for app and library resources)

Chiastic Structure/Chiasm - Chiasm is a literary device in which a sequence of ideas is presented and developed, and then repeated in reverse order. It is sometimes called introverted parallelism. The result is a "mirror" effect as the ideas are "reflected" back in a passage. Each idea is connected to its "reflection" by a repeated word, often in a related form. The term chiasm comes from the Greek letter chi, which looks like our letter X.

The structure of a chiasm is usually expressed through a series of letters, with each letter representing a new idea. For example, the structure ABBA refers to two ideas (A and B) repeated in reverse order (B and A). Often, a chiasm includes another idea in the middle of the repetition: ABXBA. In this structure, the two ideas (A and B) are repeated in reverse order, but a third idea is inserted before the repetition (X). By virtue of its position, the insertion is emphasized. Chiasm is found in verses, paragraphs, chapters, or even books of the Bible. Chiastic patterns rightly discerned, as other literary features of scripture, are an integral part of the revelation of the Word of God, so recognizing these patterns is not superimposing something artificial on the text; rather, we are discovering features of the Word as the Lord has written it. For those who want to follow closely the train of thought of Scripture, then attention to structure is essential. Parallel units will help interpret each other. The middle section draws out the main point and usually leaves us in no doubt as to what the passage is all about.

Eisegesis - the process of interpreting the text in such a way as to introduce one's own presuppositions, agendas, or biases. It is commonly referred to as "reading into the text."

Exegesis - Exegesis is a legitimate interpretation that "reads out of" the text what the original author meant to convey. Exegesis involves the careful, systematic study of the Scripture to discover the original, intended meaning. This is primarily a historical task. It is the attempt to hear the text as the original recipients were to have heard it.

Hermeneutics - Hermeneutics is the study of the principles and methods of interpreting the text of the Bible.

Parenesis - Parenesis is advice, counsel, or exhortation. They are imperatives. Often found in New Testament letters, normally as a list of instructions or exhortations. It's important to read and interpret these imperatives in the context of the main point or theme the author is making in that particular book or passage. The expression of living out these exhortations in our lives is always fueled by the gospel at work in us and in the power of the Holy Spirit. Although no consensus yet exists, a large number of scholars now view paraenesis in terms of its social function, as an amicable reminder of moral practices entailed by agreed-upon convictions. (Examples: Romans 12:9-21; Ephesians 4:25-32; 1 Peter 4:7-11)

Preunderstanding - Preunderstanding refers to all of our preconceived notions and understandings that we bring to the text, which have been formulated, both consciously and subconsciously, before we actually study the text in detail. Preunderstanding includes specific experiences and previous encounters with the text that tend to make us assume that we already understand it. Preunderstanding is formed by both good and bad influences, some accurate and some inaccurate. It includes all that you have heard in Sunday school, at church, in Bible studies, and in your private reading of the Bible. However, preunderstandings of biblical texts are also formed by hymns and other Christian music, pop songs, jokes, art, and nonbiblical literature, both Christian and secular. Likewise, culture constantly creeps in.

SENTENCE OBSERVATIONS

Repetition of Words/Phrases (Examples in 2 Corinthians 1:3-7, John 15:1-10, 1 Corinthians 15:50-54)
Look for words or phrases that repeat. How many times is it repeated in the verses you are studying? Is this word or term repeated in the surrounding context? Does the repeated word always serve the same function? Does the repeated word/phrase have the same meaning each time it occurs?

Contrasts (Examples in Proverbs 15:1, Romans 6:23, Ephesians 5:8, 1 John 1: 5-7)
Look for contrasts. Contrasts focus on differences. What word signals the contrast? What ideas, individuals, or items are being contrasted?
Common Signal Words for Contrast: *although, besides, but, compared with, even though, furthermore, more than, otherwise, rather than, though, unless, unlike, while, yet*

Comparisons (Examples in James 3:3-6, Isaiah 40:31)
Look for comparisons. Comparisons focus on similarities. What word signals the comparison? What ideas, individuals, or items are being compared?
Common Signal Words for Comparison *also, as well as, both, in the same way, in addition, just as, like, similarly, the same as, too*

Lists (Example in 1 John 2:16)
When you see more than two itemized things, you are observing a list. How many items are in the list? What items are in the list? Is there any significance to how the items are grouped?

Cause and Effect (Examples in Psalm 13:6, John 3:16, Colossians 3:1)
Look for cause-and-effect relationships. Does the cause have one effect or more than one? What is the cause and effect you note in the sentence?

Conjunctions (Examples in Romans 6:23, Hebrews 12:1, Colossians 3:12, 2 Timothy 1:7-8)
Conjunctions hold our phrases and sentences together. What function does the conjunction serve—connecting (and), contrasting (but), or concluding (therefore)?
Common Signal Words for Conjunctions: *and, for, but, therefore, since, because*

Verbs (Examples in Ephesians 4:2-3, Colossians 3:1, Ephesians 1:11, Genesis 12:3)
Verbs communicate the action of the sentence. List the verbs in the verse. Identify the tense of the verb: past, present, future, etc. What is the "voice" of the verb: active or passive? Is the verb an imperative (a command)? Who is the subject of the verb?

Figures of Speech (Examples in Psalm 119:105, Matthew 23:27)
Figures of speech are when images are communicated with words used in a sense other than the normal, literal sense. Visualize the image that is communicated in the sentence(s).

Pronouns (Example in Philippians 1:27-30)
Pronouns take the place of nouns. Identify the pronouns and the noun they replace.

"BIG 6" QUESTIONS: WHO, WHAT, WHERE, WHEN, WHY & HOW

- Who are the people in the text?
- What is happening in the text?
- What are the events taking place?
- What is the point being made?
- When did the events in the passage take place?
- Where is this taking place?
- How did this occur? How are people/places connected?
- Why is this included? Why does this person say that? Why is this important?

PARAGRAPH OBSERVATIONS

General to Specific. The author begins with a general statement, followed by the specifics explaining this thought. What is the overview/summary/general statement in the passage? What are the specifics that support the general statement?

Questions and Answers. The author uses a question-and-answer dialogue to make a point. Is the question rhetorical? Who asked the question? Was the question answered?

Dialogue. Dialogue overlaps with the question-answer feature above. Who are the participants? What is the setting? Is the setting public or private? What is the spirit of the dialogue (argument, lecture, discussion)? What is the objective of the dialogue?

Purpose/Result Statements. These phrases or sentences describe the reason, the result, or the consequences of some action. Identify the purpose/result statement.
Common Signal Words for purpose/result statements: *that, so that, in order that, or an infinitive (to+verb) that acts as a descriptor.*

Means. When an action, result, or purpose is stated, look for the means that brings about that action, result, or purpose. Answers the question: what is the means by which something is accomplished? Identify the person or object accomplishing an action, result, or purpose.

Conditional Clauses. These clauses present the conditions (introduced by "if") by which some action, consequence, reality, or result (introduced by an explicit or implied "then") will happen. What is the conditional clause (if)? What is the result clause (then)?

Action/Roles of People and of God. What are the actions/roles of people? What are the actions/ roles of God? What is the relationship between God's action/role and the action/role of people?

Emotional Terms. The Bible is a book about relationships—primarily between God and people. Note words in the text that convey feeling and emotion. What words have emotional overtones? What words are relational?

Tone. Consider the observations you've made, especially the emotional terms, and identify the tone. What is the overall tone of the passage?

DISCOURSES (units of connected text longer than paragraphs)

Connections between Paragraphs and Episodes. How do the paragraph and episode connect with the paragraphs/episodes that come before and after the one you are studying? Look for repeated words and themes. Identify logical connections. Note conjunctions between paragraphs. Pay attention to the time sequence.

Story Shifts: Major Breaks and Pivots. Look for critical places where the story seems to take a new turn. Major breaks occur in letters. Pivot episodes occur in narratives. In letters pay attention to verbs. In narratives pay attention to important choices made by characters.

Interchange. A literary device that contrasts or compares two stories at the same time as part of the overall story development. Pay attention when the narrator flows effortlessly between telling two stories. Stories organized in this way are meant to interpret one another.

Chiasm. A list of items, ideas, or events structured in a way that the first items parallels the last time, the second time parallels the next to last item, etc. Search for repeated words, similar ideas, contrasted ideas. Is there a center to the chiasm which contains the central idea?

Inclusio. A literary technique in which a passage has the same or a similar word, statement, event or theme at the beginning and the end. Pay attention to similar words, statements, events, or themes that occur at the beginning and end of an episode. Inclusios may span many chapters!

Made in the USA
Columbia, SC
29 September 2024

42644024R00041